IMAGES
of England

HUCKNALL
LOOKING BACK

Hucknall parish church, 1888. The headstone on the left bears the name Jane Harrison aged 38 years. The photographer was R.A. Bramley of The Byron Studio, 49a High Street. He advertised on the back of this cabinet print that copies could be enlarged and finished in oil, watercolour or crayon.

IMAGES
of England

HUCKNALL
LOOKING BACK

Compiled by
Harry Smith

TEMPUS

Tempus Publishing Limited
The Mill, Brimscombe Port,
Stroud, Gloucestershire, GL5 2QG

ISBN 0 7524 2067 4

Typesetting and origination by
Tempus Publishing Limited
Printed in Great Britain by
Midway Clark Printing, Wiltshire

This book is for John and Ann

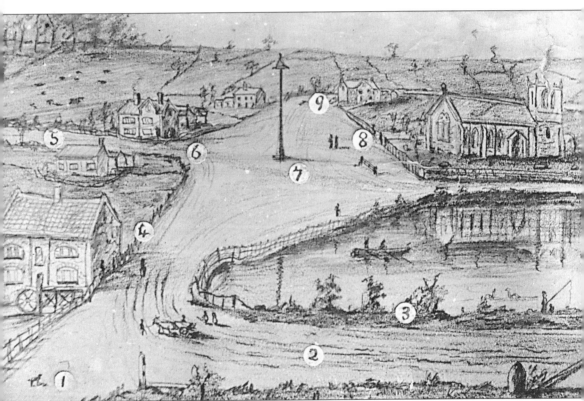

This is how the centre of Hucknall may have appeared in the Middle Ages. Looking from Carlingford Road, the mill dam (owned in 1331 by Ralph de Crumwell) is in the foreground and the church is shown as it was in 1340, with the parsonage beyond. On the left is Crumwell's water mill, (now Mill Yard) adjoining the manor house of the Rollestons. Across the road (High Street) is the manor house of the Curtis family. On the Green (Market Place) are the maypole and stocks.

Contents

Acknowledgements

Grateful thanks are due to the following friends:
Joan Bullock, the late Gwen Sisson, E.C. 'Cis' Rhodes, Renée Burrows, Geoff Breedon, Valerie and Eric Lummus, Roland Clarke, Tony Gandy and Philip Smith, for the loan of their family photographs and my special thanks to David Henshaw for producing the drawings.

The Green Memorial. (David Henshaw)

Introduction

Hucknall is pleasantly situated in the valley of the River Leen, a tributary of the River Trent seven miles North East of Nottingham. It is reasonable to suppose that the embryonic Hucknall was a Saxon settlement, an offspring of the cave dwelling mother settlement of Nottingham. The foundation of Hucknall is generally believed to lie in the twelfth century but the late Canon Gerard Barber found evidence for an early Saxon church that may be as far back as the ninth century, having discovered foundations for it in 1938. Also in 1938 the foundations of a larger nave and chancel were discovered. These finds are well documented in his book *Byron and Where he is Buried* published just before the Second World War in June 1939.

The earliest settlers might have dwelt in huts around what is now Baker Street which in time became the village green and eventually the market place. In time, a hamlet came into existence followed by the town.

The site of the present market place was always the centre of Hucknall in close association with the parish church. In the fourteenth century, a large dam, three acres in extent, dominated the site of what was much later to become the Co-operative central premises. The dam was fed from the town brook which turned the water wheel of the corn mill which was situated on the site now occupied by the Central Methodist church. The dam was originally owned by Alexander Gonaldston, who sold it, in 1331, to Richard de Crumwell who considerably enlarged it. When Ogle Street was being made, a steam-roller sank deep into the bed of clay which had previously been the dam. Nearby was the connery, the town rabbit warren, and the pinfold which was set apart to enclose stray cattle and sheep.

On the right hand side of the village green, leading from the church gates, two cottages once stood. In one lived Dr Frost, a general practitioner. The cottages were demolished when the public library was built in 1887. Two cottages on the other side, adjoining the wall of the churchyard, were removed when the church chancel was extended in 1888. In one of the cottages lived a William Calladine who witnessed the funeral of the poet Lord Byron. A stone bridge carried Baker Street over the town brook to the North Road which is now Annesley Road leading out of the town. The village stocks, designed to accommodate two persons, were positioned on the site of the present public library.

It is believed that on a site near to the Church was a manor house and also a house for the priest. The village green was also where the lord of the manor held his court of justice, where local affairs were discussed and the May Day and Patronal Festivals (or Wakes) were celebrated. Nearby was the village bakehouse in what was originally named Bakers' Lane (now Baker Street).

On 11 August 1873, a meeting of principal Hucknall tradesmen appointed Thomas Hardy (a founder of the local Co-operative Society), Peter Howis, a dealer in hardware, and James Jackson, collector of the district rate,

'to wait upon the board to make inquiry what course would be necessary to take towards establishing a Public Market – whether the necessary steps could be taken by the Local Board or if it was the duty of the ratepayers. The Board reported it was the duty of the ratepayers'! It was resolved on 9 March 1874 that 'no person be allowed to sell or vend for more than six consecutive days and no person be permitted to sell on Sundays'.

A total of £60 was collected from stallholders in tolls or rent in the financial year 1876/7 and £80 in the year 1880/1. By 1936, the tolls were bringing in a little more than £728 per annum. Today, the stall charges stand at £16.50 per day, creating a revenue of around £73,000 per annum. An average of eighty five stallholders take space each week.

The Market House which stood on the Market Place at the Baker Street Ogle Street corner, was occupied by John Critchley who operated the weighbridge adjoining in Baker Street. The last tenant was J.H. Parkin who was the rate collector.

A stone horse trough on the Baker Street side of the Market served a useful purpose for many years. It was removed to the Bulwell boundary where it was broken up during road repairing and is buried under the A611 at that spot. The Duchess of Portland who took an interest in these things described it as an early 'act of vandalism'. A cattle market at the Ogle Street side proved unsuccessful and became the 'pitching' end, used by salesmen who shouted their wares. The language was often described as 'colourful'. Market characters included 'Mad Harry', Mr Gold, who sold cure-all potions, 'Pot' Bailey who sold crockery and Alfie Donner and Frank Yexley who sold anything and everything, Nellie Stevenson sold second-hand clothing, Rabin, Nottingham lace, Florrie Ford was famed for her lace curtains and nets and Gypsy Wilson sold linoleum.

The Wakes Fair used the Market Place until 1926 when it transferred to the Albert Street recreation ground. Bostock and Wombwells menagerie was always an attraction. In recent years it has returned to its origins.

The beginning of the nineteenth century saw Hucknall with little prominence in the industrial sense. Indeed Papplewick, by way of its cotton mills on the River Leen being far superior in that it employed hundreds of people. By the middle of the nineteenth century the population was just over 2,000 and nearly all were employed in agriculture, stocking making or at the Papplewick Mills.

About this time, the Shetland Shawl industry came to the town and a few years later (1860), the sinking of the pits and the expansion of the coal industry heralded the making of modern Hucknall with people coming to the town from all parts of the country to find employment and share in its prosperity.

The town continued to prosper through the twentieth century contributing by way of its coal resources, aeronautical expertise (Rolls Royce) and manpower in agriculture, industry and the armed forces in two world wars. The coming of a nationalised coal industry and the expansion of the textile and light engineering trades ensured Hucknall became a prosperous town until in recent years the demise of 'King Coal' and recession in the textile trade has brought a drastic change in economic fortunes. Many famous, local business names have been lost in recent years including, Viyella, Vedonis, Jaeger, Bonser Engineering, Fanfare Displays, Highfield Productions, W. Reynolds & Co. and The Hanmade Co. Ltd.

It is perhaps significant that the Shetland Shawl and stocking trades in the form of The Hucknall Manufacturing Co. and F.J. Bamkin, which were introduced into Hucknall so long ago in the town's history still prosper. They have survived and overseen so many changes in the commercial aspect of the town. We hope their success heralds the coming of a new era in the future prosperity of the town.

Over the years Hucknall has been fortunate to have had some excellent photographers among its townsfolk. Among the most notable were Dr Harrison Coates, Claude and Deryck Bullock and Walter North. Photographs from all of them appear in this book and without them such a book would not have been possible. The book does not aspire to be in any way a history of the town, we have that already from eminent local historians such as J.H. Beardsmore, Canon Barber and Eric Horriben. What the book does do is to provide a vivid pictorial look at the town from a period beginning in the latter part of the nineteenth century and continuing through to the middle years of the twentieth century. The photographs have been selected, in the main, from the Eric and Henry Morley family archive, supplemented by generous contributions from family and friends. It is my hope, that *Hucknall Looking Back*, will provide a nostalgic journey for the reader and revive many happy memories of Hucknall as it used to be.

Harry Smith
Southwell
July 2000

One
High Street and the Town

With good reason, Hucknall mothers used to instruct their children to 'keep off the hoss-road'.
Here is a High Street traffic jam before the motorcar took over.

Portland Road, now High Street, 1855. The gate on the left marks the entrance to a farmyard. The National Provincial Bank now occupies this site. On the right is the Old Box Tree, reputed to be 600 years old.

A similar view of Portland Road, 1889. The gentleman standing at the shop doorway marks what eventually became 'Pat' Griffin's barber's shop.

A very early view looking down the High Street from the church tower.

Annesley Road and Baker Street corner showing the Central Co-op store in the early years of the twentieth century. This site is still occupied by the Society's hall and shops but is now sadly empty and neglected.

A typical Hucknall dwelling on Portland Road in the 1890s when agriculture was the main occupation in the area.

Taylor's Buildings, Portland Road disappeared in May 1938 under a demolition order made by the Council.

A house called Wighay Nook which stood just beyond the Wighay Bridge on Annesley Road. The premises were demolished in the late 1930s to make way for The Hucknall Co-operative Society shops which still exist and are occupied by private tenants.

A multi-view postcard showing five scenes in Hucknall as it once was.

Hucknall Old Manor House showing the front aspect to High Street, 1930s. The shop on the left was at that time occupied by Johnstone the butcher and the one to the right, the town toy shop owned by Mr Allcock.

The rear view of the Old Manor House facing what is now the Yorke Street car park, 1930s.

A quaint old corner of Hucknall showing Millott's Yard, off High Street, opposite Vine Terrace as these cottages appeared before demolition in the 1930s. It took its name from the Millott family, one of some standing in the district One of the members of the family was a Freeman of the City of London.

The Malthouse Mill Yard at the junction of Annesley Road and Baker Street in 1946.

An excellent study of High Street corner prior to re-devolopment. Stallard's shoe-shop just edges on to the right side of the scene next to the passage entrance to the Half Moon public house. Who would dare to stand in this road to-day? The photographer added a name to this picture postcard – 'Bottleneck, Hucknall'.

High Street leading to the Market. Christian the tailor, Whyatt the fruiterer, The old Byron's Rest inn (selling Nottingham Brewery Ales), Heath the chemist and Stallard's shoe shop are among the buildings in the view.

Part of the nineteenth-century High Street looking towards the Market Place, which was the first part of Hucknall to receive a twentieth-century face-lift. On the left is A.W. Saxton's electrical shop, Johnstone's butchers shop and Allcock's toyshop.

Looking towards the Market Place in the early part of the twentieth century when the Zachariah Green monument was still in its original place.

The Hucknall public library which was a gift to the town by Messrs, Ellis and Paget. The section on the left was the librarian's house. The decorations are for the Coronation of King George VI in 1937.

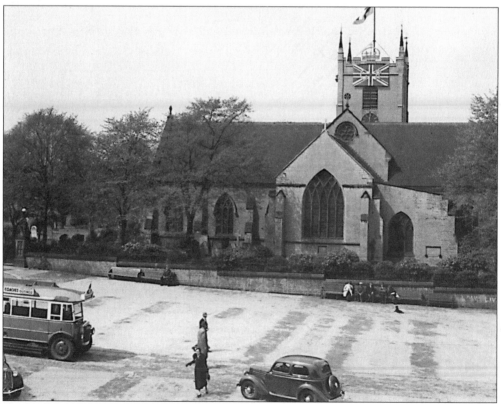

Hucknall market place and the parish church. The church tower is adorned for the coronation in 1937.

Baker Street from the church tower showing the chimney of the blacksmiths forge which can be seen next to E. & J. Lowe the estate agents.

The Scala cinema seen from an unusual aspect, the church tower. The former billiard and snooker hall, in the middle view, is now known as The Lord Byron public house. The National School playing field can be seen to the left of the picture and in the far distance is Linby Colliery.

This winter scene on the Market Place with stalls being erected in the snow reminds us of a period when life was not quite so hectic.

Hucknall cattle market in the summer of 1904. 'Why be dependent on Nottingham?', the butchers asked. At the first market the first beast sold was a fine specimen entered by Sir Charles Seely and knocked down to Mr G. Elkington for £29 15s 0d. Such an auspicious occasion was not to be passed without a banquet. Sadly, in spite of all the good wishes and intentions, the market faded within a few weeks, never to be resurrected.

The Byron's Rest public house at the bottom of Chapel Street prior to demolition. The funeral cortège of the poet was reputed to have rested there before laying the body to rest in the family vault in the parish church. This was most unlikely as the funeral procession approached the town down the North Road (now Annesley Road). There was no main road into the town from Nottingham at that time and the cortège arrived behind schedule in the late afternoon.

The Coffee Tavern, High Street, now shop premises, seen here in the 1920s.

Looking up High Street from the Byron Cinema. The lorry in the foreground is that of Haslams mineral water manufacturers. The sign of C.A. Cash can be seen on the left. The hardware shop of J. Lodge is on the right whilst The Chequers Inn can be seen top right. The photograph was probably taken in the late 1930s.

Baker Street Corner – an early phase in the removal of the 'bottle neck' in 1938. Taylor's fish shop is about to disappear.

This was the Chapel Street junction with High Street – 'the bottle-neck' A pedestrian glances back to look as demolition gets under way. Note the advertisement for Misk Health Salts.

Baker Street corner demolition is well advanced. All the work is being carried out by hand, apart from the horse being used to haul the salvage away. Notice that no-one even wears a protective helmet. Jacksons pork shop was to survive this phase, along with what became Hilda Peppers sweet shop.

Two workmen on the roof with heavy hammers are watched by a lone pedestrian. J. Coleman, Gramophone and Records, moved to Annesley Road, close to John Wilmott's present day premises.

Baker Street corner thirty years later, in 1968.

A new shop for A.W. Saxton is being built behind the old one. On the door of the old shop it reads, 'accumalators charged'. What would owners of early radios have done without this service?

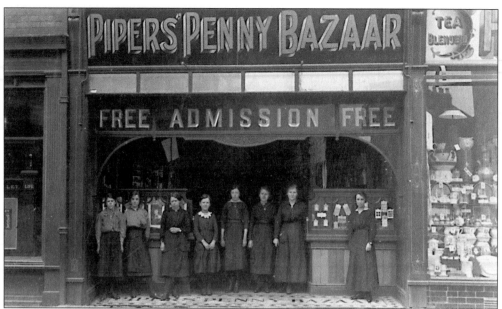

Pipers' Penny Bazaar was opposite where Barclay's Bank is now. In this photograph, from around 1916, the member of staff third from the right is Nancy Breedon(née Brown).

Hilda Pepper's shop on High Street at the corner of Albert Street. Nancy Brown also worked here, she is on the left and Mrs Pepper is holding her baby son Walter. The property was sold to F.W. Woolworth and Mrs Pepper moved to Baker Street where she continued to trade for many years.

Wilcockson's butchers shop and family house in Baker Street, 1895. The boys are brothers, Robert and Owen Wilcockson. The property was redeveloped around 1900 but there remained a butchers shop on the site until 1997. At the moment it is occupied by the Crystal Cavern, and the laundrette next door is owned and managed by Clare Hancock, grand daughter of Owen Wilcockson. The shuttered cottage on the right still stands today and is used by Bell's Taxis. This may be one of the oldest surviving properties in the town

Benjamin Clay stands with his son Cyril outside their Annesley Road butchers shop in 1914. The business has continued in the same family for over one hundred years. Derrick and Dorothy Clay still provide an excellent service to the townspeople of Hucknall today.

Station Road and High Street corner showing J. Cupit's newsagent and tobacconists shop now owned by Eddie Johnson. The large thermometer at the entrance of the shop was a familiar sight in the 1930s as it was a popular advertisement for Stephens Ink. The Co-operative shop next door is now a Sports Shop owned by Mr Dereck Day. The photograph was taken in 1935.

Mr W. Musson's shop in High Street opposite The Derbyshire Building Society. The proprietor is on the left, Cecil Bowd is in the centre and Florrie Wagg is on the extreme right.

The family grocery and provision business of J. Rickett in Watnall Road was typical of the many small family shops that provided variety and choice for shoppers in Hucknall in the first half of the twentieth century. Like everywhere else family businesses like this one began to decline as the larger stores and supermarkets of the post-war years started to appear. Opposite this shop was the showroom of C.B. Munks.

Christmas is the time for toys and it was to this shop that people went to buy them in Hucknall. Mr 'Toy' Allcock sold a fine range of goods to delight the younger generation (see p. 71).

Demolition in progress at the Cigar Factory, Hankin Street in the 1960s Winson's general grocery can be seen next to the factory which, for many years, was occupied by Sidney Davis, Family Butcher. The new council houses can be seen at the end of the road and Bottom Pit's spoil heaps beyond.

The remains of Eastwell Street, viewed from Spring Street, c. 1955. Annesley Road can just be seen and Brook Street is on the extreme right. Darlison Court now occupies the void on the corner.

Annesley Road at the bottom gate of Annesley Park showing the gamekeeper's cottage and also the man who opened the gate for traffic in 1903.

Annesley Road at the same spot many years later. Road widening and resurfacing is taking place in this photograph of 1971.

Victoria Cottages, Broomhill prior to road widening in the late 1950s.

Broomhill House, Nottingham Road was a house of character and the former home of Mr and Mrs E.H. Story. It was finally the home of Mr and Mrs Vaughan Radford before becoming The Bowman Hotel and Restaurant.

Two
Civil and Military Events

The 'Official Party' at the Market Place, including Cllrs 'Dingy' Spencer and William Calladine, await the arrival of King George V for his visit to the town in 1914.

Crowds on Baker Street await the arrival of King George V on 25 June 1914. It appears that the water cart has passed by to wet the roads and so damp down the dust before His Highness's visit.

'Fear God and Honour The King' is the slogan on the banner adorning the High Street for the visit of the King. Numerous policeman, who are apparently wearing special sashes for the occasion, are in place to control the crowds who wait patiently for the arrival of their monarch. Meanwhile the grocery shop on the right advertises, 'Finest preserving sugar', just right for all that soft fruit that must have been arriving in the shops and growing in the gardens.

This may have been the scene after the King had passed this way because the crowds are now dispersing and just a few people are left in the streets, discussing the events of the day and dressed in their best. The man on the left of the group, without a hat, appears to be Mr Allcock from the toyshop.

Watnall Road is ready for the King's visit: the Union Flag flies over the Council Offices and banners and bunting span the street. Roads have been closed to traffic and a few dignitaries wait in the middle of the street for their proud moment to arrive – tension mounts!

Hucknall Military Tribunal in session in March 1916. The members of the tribunal were, from left to right, back row: F.W. Raynor, J. Foster, W.J. Calladine JP, H. Spencer, W. Moss. Front row: W. Sowter (reporter), T.S. Adamson (reporter), R.B. Gandy (jnr clerk), H. Gandy (acting clerk to the Tribunal), C.H. Hill JP (military representative). Dick Gandy, the junior clerk and son of H. Gandy, eventually became treasurer to the town, a position he carried out with 'the utmost efficiency and decorum'. The inset shows R.B. (Dick) Gandy much later, with his own son, Tony.

Like many towns in Britain Hucknall did not build a Cenotaph until several years after the First World War so this 'Shrine', situated at the bottom of Duke Street, was where the townspeople placed their tributes to the fallen.

Ex-Servicemen marching to Broomhill House from the Market Place, after laying their floral tributes at 'The Shrine'. They were entertained at Broomhill to tea in a marquee. The shop of Howis, ironmonger and plumber, fronts both High Street and Watnall Road.

Peace celebrations in the Market Place in 1919. The business premises from left to right are: the Ogle Street frontage of the Scala cinema, Geo. Shepherd, undertaker, The Byron Buildings,

Byron Chip Saloon, Colonial Meat Stores and, on the Market Place, itself, the public convenience.

The people of the town along with 'the boys that came' back pay their respects as they march past 'The Shrine'. The farm on the left and the hoardings are now the site of the Byron cinema and The Salvation Army building.

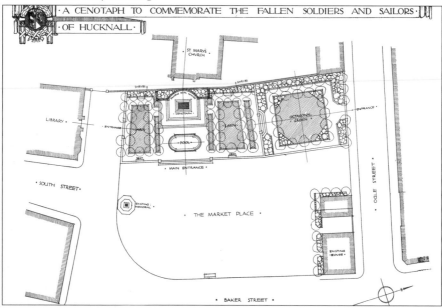

A CENOTAPH TO COMMEMORATE THE FALLEN SOLDIERS AND SAILORS OF HUCKNALL

What Might Have Been. It is not well known that immediately after the First World War, an elaborate scheme for a memorial in the Market Place was planned and the distinguished Hucknall architect, Mr T. Cecil Howitt, prepared this outline plan. It was not proceeded with, but the Cenotaph, designed by Mr, Howitt, was later built at Titchfield Park. The 'existing memorial' refers to the Green Memorial, later removed to Titchfield Park. The 'existing house' was occupied by the late Mr J.H. Parkin, rate collector, and the building next to it was the public convenience. Both of these were later demolished.

The unveiling of The Cenotaph in Titchfield Park on 3 September 1922 The inset shows Brig. General Sir J.F. Laycock who unveiled the memorial.

Duchess Of Portland Laying Stone
St Peter's Church April 25 1892 Hucknall

The Duchess of Portland laying the foundation stone of St Peter's church, Watnall Road on 25 April 1892. The Sandy Lane windmill can just be discerned in the distance.

An historic photograph recording the scene at the ceremony which marked the unveiling of the Zachariah Green memorial fountain at the Market Place in 1898.

The Duke of Portland gifted Titchfield Park to the town to mark the coming of age of his heir. The land was originally given in 1914 but the Great War delayed its development. Titchfield Park opened in July 1922. Pictured left to right are: J.W. Bardill (contractor), The Marquise and Marchioness of Titchfield (who performed the opening ceremony), W.J. Calladine, A. Plumb and police Sergeant Whitsed.

The Duke of York, who later became King George VI, opening The Homes of Rest at Park Drive in February 1926. On his right is Mr Joseph Barker, former headmaster of Spring Street school, and on his left is Sir Julian Cahn.

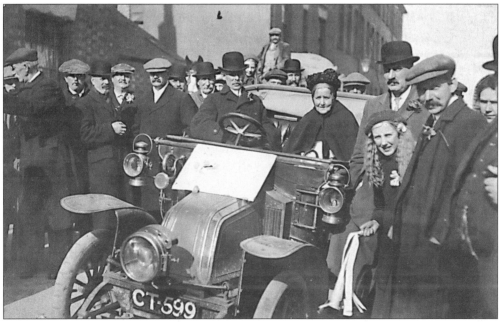

Mrs Ullyatt, who lived to be ninety-three, pictured arriving to cast her vote at the Butlers Hill school polling station in 1913 when she was ninety. The driver of the car is Mr W. Moss.

The first Civic Parade on 24 April 1921. Cllr A. Plumb JP revived the custom on being elected Chairman of The Council. It seems everyone wore a hat or cap in those days.

The Civic Parade moving along High Street after assembling at the Market Place. One shop is advertising pure butter at 2s 6d per lb.

Hucknall Urban District Council members in 1927. (Photograph Walter North)

A group of Hucknall councillors with friends in the 1920s. Third from right on the front row is Mr Joseph Barker who at the time was headmaster of Spring Street school. Mr Moss is far left, W.J. Calladine fifth from left and Herbert Plumb tenth from left.

Laying the foundation stone at the Watnall Road Welfare Centre on 4 April 1936. Standing at the front left is Dr Walter Garstang and facing him, wearing his badge of office, is Cllr W. (Billy) Mee, Chairman of Hucknall Urban District Council.

The official proclamation of George V1 as king from the balcony of the Hucknall Public Hall in 1937. The Public Hall was built in 1875 at a cost of £2,000 to seat 550 people. The balcony has not been used for an official purpose since this event. The hall was transformed into offices by Hucknall Urban District Council and after the merger with Ashfield, the building was sold to a private owner.

The centenary of Byron's death on 19 April 1924 was marked by a special service at the parish church. The people in the main group, starting from the second lady on the left, are: Mrs C. Daws, Mrs L. Smedley, Mr W. Moss (in the top hat), Mr H. Gandy, Mr J.G. Slater (Chairman of the Council, with wreath), Mr C. Clarke, Mr A. Plumb (holding hat), Mr W. Jacklin and Mr C. Northfield.

An imposing looking group photographed outside the Welfare Centre, Watnall Road in the early years of the twentieth century. Unfortunately we do not know what this event was all about, although the gentleman on the extreme left is known to be Mr W. Moss.

Officials and dignitaries at the Kings Cup Air Race at Hucknall Aerodrome in the 1930s Cllr Ira H. Buck is at the microphone.

Three
Church Activities

A Baptist church ladies' sewing party, *c.* 1910. In the group are, from left to right, back row: mesdames, S. Johnson, H. Noble, G. Davy, T. Roome, G. Richardson, A. Severn, ? Doughty, J. Bodill, H. Critchley. Middle row: ? Kiddy, J. Clarke, E. Hobbs, ? Carpenter, W. Joynes, T. Hewitt, ? Booth, ? Parkin, ? Taylor. Bottom row: H. Briggs, F. Hardstaff, W. Joynes, W. Whyatt, I. Buck, R. Morley.

The Gilbert Street chapel was the meeting place of the Hucknall Baptists before they moved to their present church on Watnall Road. The rear of the premises fronts Derbyshire Lane and this spot has for many years been used as a car maintenance and repair shop.

William Calladine (1826-1895) moved to Hucknall from Melbourne in Derbyshire. He played a tremendous part in the development of the Baptist church. The sincerity of his religious convictions were expressed in service to the community and development of the town. He and his family lived in the precincts of the parish church. Their house abutted the east end. He took an active part in politics and was instrumental in forming the Co-operative movement.

An interestingt-looking group of local notables, c. 1920. Standing on the left is J.H. Beardsmore next to Canon Barber and standing on the right is C.S. Harris, schoolmaster. Mrs Barber is seated on the left and Mrs Chaworth Musters holds the bouquet. (Photograph Walter North)

A younger Canon Barber (seated, centre) with a church group from the early 1900s. Schoolmaster William Jacklin is on Canon Barber's left and on his right is Miss Fieldhouse. The Revd Eling (curate) stands at the centre back. Notice also that two members of the group have been added by the photographer after the picture was taken. They stand out because they are not quite to the same scale!

The Vicar of Hucknall teaches an interested young audience in the parish church porch in 1954. The Revd K.G. Thompson became the first Bishop of Sherwood. Born in 1909, he died in 1975. Was there a budding priest in this audience?

A drawing of Hucknall church from the West Street gate entrance. (David Henshaw)

A group of church elders by the church porch in 1907, the year Canon Barber was instituted as Vicar of Hucknall. From left to right, standing: Messrs I. Shephard (evangelist), F. Winfield (church warden), E. Bostock (verger). Seated: Mr W. Jacklin (church warden and schoolmaster), the Reverends S.G.O. Anderson (curate), T.G. Barber, Rees Jones (Saint John's), T.H.J. Eling (Saint Peter's).

On the 14 August 1926 the former King George and Queen Elisabeth of Greece came to Hucknall to pay tribute to the memory of the poet Lord Byron. Both laid wreaths on the tomb. Left to right: The ex-Queen of Greece, Sir H. Bowden, Canon Barber, and the ex-King of Greece. (Photograph Walter North)

Newstead Abbey became the property of The City of Nottingham in July 1931 the gift of Sir Julien Cahn (framed, on the right, in the car window). The Greek President Venizelos, attended the ceremonies. This photograph shows the President being welcomed by Canon Barber at the parish church. (Photograph Walter North)

"Veniselos at Hucknall.(W.N.)

The children of Hucknall give an enthusiastic welcome as the President of Greece walks to the church entrance. Canon Barber looks a little more serious! (Photograph Walter North)

The Greek President lays the first of many wreaths on the poet's tomb in July 1931.

The full display of floral tributes to the poet in the parish church after the ceremony. The one from Missolonghi is particularly significant because that is where Byron died.

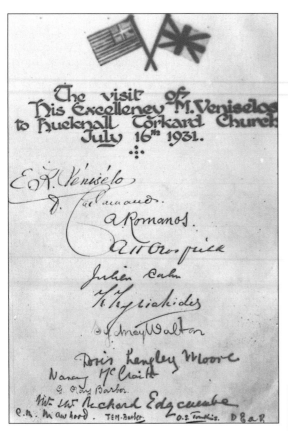

The church visitors' book. The Greek President's signature tops the list. Sir Julien Cahn's name is easily readable along with that of Doris Langley Moore, well known to Byron enthusiasts for her writings on the poet.

The tablet to the memory of the poet in the parish church placed there by his sister Augusta Mary Leigh.

A happy group of Baptist church members embarking on a charabanc outing to the east coast, the open top denotes optimism for good weather ahead! Warner's Café is in the background. Just in view on the right is the chemists shop of J.H. Harmon. At the far left of the picture is Eric Morley and, standing (hatless) behind the vehicle, is Harold Calladine.

Father MacDonnel came to Hucknall after the building of the Carlingford Road Catholic church. According to his description in the 1939 diamond jubilee souvenir booklet, he was 'a short, stout, good-natured man, jovial and sincere. He worked hard and unselfishly to promote firm friendship with everyone.'

A group of Baptist church thespians dressed for their presentation of *Bunyan the Dreamer* in the 1920s. Harold Calladine is on the extreme left, holding a sword, Eric and Harry Morley can be seen on the back row, left of centre, with staffs. Hannah Cooke stands next to Harold Calladine. Wilson Buck is in the centre and the vicar on the right is Revd Woodeson. (Photograph Claude Bullock)

The Baptish church, 'Ruffles' concert party, *c.* 1930. Back row, left is Miss Hannah Cooke, second left Eric Morley. Seated, left is Roy Walker and second left Eric Johnson. Miss Dorothy Plumb is seated on the right.

Four

Transport

Nottingham based brewery Home Ales deliver to the Bee Hive off licence in High Street. Note that the beer is arriving in large wooden casks. As a single deck bus squeezes past the brewer's vehicle a council workman is engaged in gully cleansing but without the powered machinery of today.

Linby Pit Top in 1880, illustrating the very simple mode of transport used to access the pit bottom. The notice on the headgear states that 'not more than twelve persons to descend or ascend this shaft at one time and no boy under sixteen alone'.

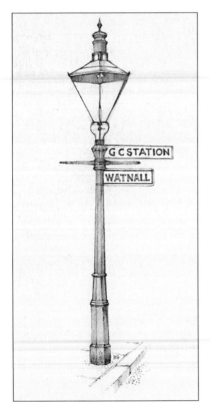

This drawing shows a gas lamp that once stood on High Street pointing the way to the Great Central Railway station and the village of Watnall. (David Henshaw)

The Hucknall Fire Brigade leave the council yard in Watnall Road at speed, with local building contractor Tom Hanson at the wheel , in the 1930s.

Probably one of the funniest pictures in Hucknall's history! This was the day, sometime around the turn of the century, when the local fire brigade turned out on a horse-drawn barrow because they could not get their engine to start. A crowd of sightseers, and dogs, follow and look on as the gallant force gallop past. The council offices are on the left. The range of services provided by Arnold's shop is impressive. As well as advertising cycle repairs and tyres for sale he was a hairdresser and tobacconist! Notice also that there is a sign for an 'Emigration Office' next door to the shop on the right.

Breedon and Wightman's garage, Portland Road in the 1930s. Mr E. Breedon is on the right of the picture wearing a cap and C.G. Wightman, sporting a trilby, stands on the other side of the truck. The star signs demonstrate that Texaco motor oil was available from this garage and an impressive line-up of 1930s commercial vehicles complete the view.

Staff of Trent Motor Traction Company at the company garage in Portland Road in the early 1930s. Foreman Bill Stubbins is fifth from the right.

Nothing changes! Traffic chaos in the 1970s on Annesley Road at the junction with Allan Street.

Starting this 1930s Trent bus the old-fashioned way with a turn of the handle, was obviously not a problem to this well dressed gentleman with a button hole flower. The lady looking on had obviously been busy with the hair tongs before venturing out!

A Stevenson's Transport lorry ploughs through the heavy rain in this atmospheric 1930s picture of the High Street. Jackson's Pork Butchers can be seen on the left.

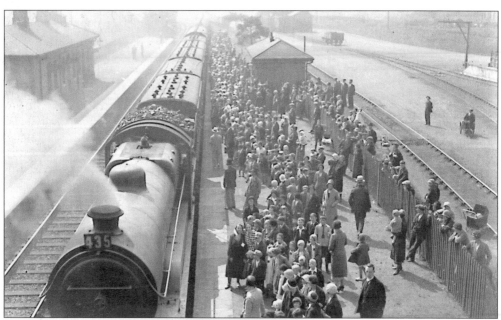

Remember the excitement of an early morning wait on the platform for the train that would take you to the seaside? This is a British Legion children's outing to Bridlington seen as they are just about to board the train from Hucknall Town station in 1935. It looks as though they were in for a sunny day too!

Five

Events and
Personalities

This illustration of the 'Hucknall Torkard Feast in 1851' is from a painting used on a postcard and sent, probably, around the turn of the twentieth century. It was published by H. Jackson of Hucknall and a short message on the back addressed to Miss Minnie Shaw, says that it will show her 'How Hucknall was when I was two', signed, H.S. Several items in the scene are worthy of note: the thatched cottage on the left was the home of 'spinsters Hannah and Mary Truman, seamstresses and herbalists' and ultimately the site of the Byrons Rest. The sign of the Half Moon can be seen. The house in the churchyard, looking down the High Street, was the home of the 'gigantic' Dr Frost (see p. 69). Houses standing on what is now the market place were those of Mr Allcock, Mr Hodges and Mr Kirk. At the corner on the right, abutting the church, was the house of Mr William Calladine, which was later a Co-operative shop. Nearby was the site of the Bee Hive stores.

Hucknall May Festival in 1876. This very early photographic survivor shows the third Hucknall May Queen and her attendants, all in splendid costumes. This sepia-tinted photograph was originally also hand coloured with watercolour, now much faded, but still showing green grass and blue and red flowers on the decorations!

The thirty fourth Hucknall May Festival in 1907. These splendidly dressed participants were photographed outside the Hucknall Nurses Home in Beardall Street.

The programme and 'Book of Words' for the Third Annual May Festival held in 1875. Music was provided by the Juvenile Band, whose unusual line-up included harp, banjo, cymbals, bones, triangle and two pianos, all played by local children! The programme began with Maypole dancing and continued with songs and recitations before the Queen and her attendants made their entrance to a 'trumpet flourish'. The day ended with the patriotic song, 'Now Pray We For Our Country'.

BOOK OF WORDS

THIRD ANNUAL

MAY FESTIVAL,

1875.

HUCKNALL TORKARD.

QUEEN - - - - MISS MARY HAWKINS.

CONDUCTOR - MR. H. BEARDSMORE.

PIANIST - MR. F. GRATION.

This group of former May Queens gathered together to celebrate the Diamond Jubilee of the event in 1933. On the right of the picture stands Mr J.H. Beardsmore the Hucknall local historian.

A cabinet portrait photograph of Ben Caunt who was born 22 March 1815 and died 10 September 1861 and was the champion prize-fighter of all England in 1842. He was buried in the parish churchyard and his grave became a place of pilgrimage in the nineteenth century, attracting more visitors than were later to visit the tomb of Lord Byron. According to former local MP William Whitlock, the great bell that strikes the hour from its tower above the Palace of Westminster, Big Ben, takes its name from him.

This is Zachariah Green (1817–1897) who was a stockinger, renowned for a 'gift of healing' and who played some part in almost every Hucknall organisation of his time. At the age of forty five, he was presented with a purse containing forty five golden guineas in recognition of his 'valuable services to healing'. His death in 1897 prompted the people of Hucknall to subscribe £400 towards the erection of a granite memorial fountain in the market place. The monument now stands on Titchfield Park. The names of several other members of the Green family who carried on the same caring healing work have since been added to the memorial. The last inscription to be added was for Mary Green who died in 1980 aged ninety-two years. The little boy in the photograph may be Zachariah's grandson.

Zachariah Arthur Green MC, LRCP, LRCS, LRFPS, 1892-1932 is the third inscription on the Green Family Monument on Titchfield Park. In June 1983, a fourth name, Mary, was added. Zachariah A.Green was the third member of the Green family to be medically orientated. After school and university he gained exceptional medical qualifications at Edinburgh. During the Great War, he served in the RAMC where for his valour in tending the wounded, he was awarded the Military Cross. After the war, he took up duties as house surgeon at Newark hospital until, after a serious illness, he returned to Hucknall. After convalescence, Doctor Green commenced practice in his home town where his charming personality and wide experience endeared him to the town's people. After a short illness 'due to overwork', he was lost to the people of Hucknall in 1932.

A memorial card for Dr John Frost, the Hucknall surgeon who lived in the cottage by the side of the church gate. He was a man of huge physique reputedly weighing 27 stones. After his death in 1864 at the age of fifty nine, his body had to be lowered on to the hearse from a bedroom window.

Above left: Hannah Ball, a Hucknall drover. This illustration from a postcard published by H. Jackson of Hucknall in the 1920s dates from the 1870s.

Above: This is 'Mrs Williamson, Impersonator', in around 1903. She performed locally as 'Mrs Farley's Waxworks' and lived at The Beehive in the High Street. These premises are now a newsagents.

Left: John Edward Ellis, was perhaps Hucknall's greatest benefactor. In a letter dated 18 March 1861, he wrote, 'on the ledge of my window lies a specimen of the first stone turned in commencing the new coal pits at Hucknall'. He stayed not only to manage this colliery, but he later presented to the town the Public Hall and the Library, built at a cost of £2,000, in 1887. He promoted an undertaking to supply Hucknall with its own pure water supply which came into being in 1881. In 1885, he was elected Member of Parliament for the Rushcliffe Parliamentary division and held the seat for twenty five years. His last gift to Hucknall was the swimming baths, in 1909. He died in December of the following year. Despite his long period of service to the town he is no longer comemorated in any public way in Hucknall today.

A favourite character with the children of Hucknall was Mr Allcock or 'Mr Toy Allcock' as he was known. The elegant-looking Mr Allcock, seen here probably in the early 1900s, kept the toy shop in the High Street. This postcard was sent to a friend as a New Year's greetings card, apparently by the man himself as it is signed, 'Kind thoughts from Mr and Mrs Allcock' and posted from an address in Mablethorpe where, perhaps, he had stayed for the holiday.

Hucknall's gift to the theatre, Robin (Bill) Bailey, photographed at the home of the late Ken Burrows of Woodford Road in 1970. Ken Burrows was responsible for the production of many of the Hucknall Dramatic Society's plays in the 1930s. In the group are, left to right: Ken Burrows, Mrs Bailey, Robin Bailey, Jean Vann and Mrs and Dr R.H. Vartan.

A production of *The Ghost Train* performed by Hucknall Dramatic Club on stage at the Church Hall in the 1930s. Plays were produced with great imagination and flair by Ken Burrows, who in this production created the illusion of a train passing through the station. The players, including Robin Bailey and Cyril and Ella Barker, entertained to full houses, performing at a near professional standard. Cyril Barker is pictured here on stage (centre left). After the Second World War, Cyril took over Ken Burrow's roll as producer, presenting play after play with the same panache as his predecessor.

Two 'newspaper shots' of Henry Morley standing on the tennis court at the rear of the Dispatch Office on Yorke Street. Henry Morley founded the *Hucknall Dispatch*, a weekly newspaper, in 1903. The competition from other local weekly papers (there were three) was enormous, and the population of Hucknall at the time was only 15,000. By 1913, only the *Dispatch* remained.

Ninety years young! Henry Morley celebrating his birthday with the 'Dispatch' staff, an event that was filmed to be shown on television. His son Harry Morley is on his immediate left. Second from the left is a young Denis Robinson.

Dr and Mrs Harrison Coates by the door of their home at Tenter Hill in Duke Street in around 1900. This extremely popular Hucknall doctor, the father of the famous composer Eric Coates, was an accomplished photographer who was responsible for some of the earliest underground photography. His passion for bull dogs was rewarded when he won the British Bull Dog Club Championship in 1898 with his entry 'Hucknall Prince.'

Eric Coates was accorded a civic welcome when he opened the town's carnival in July 1935. He is seen here with the Chairman of the Council W. Mee and members and officials in the Council Chamber, Watnall Road. Born in Hucknall in 1886, Eric Coates left the town in 1905 and achieved world-wide fame as a composer of light music. His success never diminished his love for the town of his birth and native county, returning home whenever his musical commitments allowed.

A photograph taken by Eric Morley of the composer enjoying a joke during a visit to the town of his birth.

Another Eric Morley snapshot showing the composer with his elder brother Gwn who lived on Wood Lane. Gwn stayed in Hucknall all his life and prior to retirement was the manager at Linby Colliery.

Mrs Phylis Coates unveils the plaque placed on the Hucknall home of her late husband. The plaque was presented by the Hucknall Rotary Club.

On 18 July 1946, Rannoch Lodge, Watnall Road, the home of Dr and Mrs R.H. Vartan, was the venue for the Silver Jubilee Garden Party of the Hucknall branch of the British Legion. Eric Coates performed the opening ceremony. The composer is seen as he was presented with an album of local photographs by Mr C.H. Buzzard the branch secretary. On the left of the picture is Lt Col. J.N. Chaworth-Musters and on the extreme right is Cllr S.S. Greenhalgh.

Six
Sport and Leisure

This and the next few photographs were taken by Walter North in the 1920s and illustrate the attractions of Titchfield Park in its heyday. This one shows the boating lake.

The children's sand-pit in Titchfield Park, *c.* 1920. Parties of Sunday school children would

come here for their annual outing.

The paddling pool and slide, Titchfield Park, 1920s.

The Tea Pavilion, Titchfield Park, 1920s.

The old band stand, Titchfield Park.

HUCKNALL OLD AMATEURS.F.C. 1887

Hucknall Old Amateurs Football Club in 1887.

Hucknall Primitive Methodists Cricket Club – Spencer Cup Winners 1914. The back row includes J. Dunn (umpire), Ernest Sabin. Left to right, middle row: J.H. Johnson, Billy Robinson, S. Johnson, Horace Smith, Arthur Raynor. Front row, second left is J.H. Smith.

The Scala Cinema, Annesley Road, in the 1930s. It was later used as an extension to the Co-operative Stores.

The Byron Cinema under construction in the mid-1930s. It still survives today, although divided for both movies and bingo.

The Baptist church tennis club in the 1930s. Left to right, standing: Miss Ruddock, Albert Richardson, -?-, Mrs Roy Walker, Lizzy Parking, Mr Newing, Hannah Cook, Roy Walker, Edna Morley, Harry Morley, Miss, Newing, -?-. Front row: Eric Morley, Nora Noble, -?-.

Spencer Cup Winners 1937. 'Syl' Houldsworth, in a blazer, with 'capped' Cecil and Henry Rhodes to his right, receives the trophy. K.W. (Ken) Brown can be seen at the top, extreme right. On the left of the picture, and next to the 'Pearly-King', is Bill Hodgman.

Hucknall Cricket Club, c. 1938. Left to right, back row: G. Pepper (scorer), A. Tilford, R.R.Wilcockson, F. Butterworth, S.P. Holgate, C.E. Downham, F.E. Saxton, J. Sears (umpire). Front row: D. Cale, C. Rhodes, F.W. Saxton, J.F. Johnstone. Inset: Sylvestor Houldsworth. Cecil Rhodes passed away in 1958, aged 61 years, and was described in the local press at that time as Hucknall's 'Mr Sport'. He had planned to retire from the captaincy of Hucknall Cricket Club that year having been associated with local cricket from boyhood. Frank Saxton was a great servant to Hucknall Cricket Club in particular and Nottinghamshire cricket in general which he endowed with a great talent. It was always acknowledged that the intervention of the 1939-1945 war prevented him playing at the highest level.

Hucknall Cricket Club, 1958. The club entered two teams in the Spencer Cup Competition and both reached the final. They are pictured here at Titchfield Park. Cecil Rhodes Snr is on the left (umpire) and 'Cis' Rhodes is sixth along the back row from his father. Doug Cale is third from the right standing with K.W. Brown (padded) in the centre. The little boy who scored for the game was Ian Cale.

Ernest Coleman (1908-1984) follows fellow Arsenal players George Male and Jimmy Dunne on to the field at Highbury on the 6 January 1933. The player behind Ernest Coleman is the legendary Cliff Bastin. The date is significant in the history of English football, the nation having been shocked to learn of the sudden death early that morning, of Herbert Chapman, arguably the greatest manager in the history of the national game. Ernest Coleman began his football career with Hucknall church Lads Brigade, turning professional with Halifax Town and enjoying a distinguished career with Grimsby Town, Arsenal, Middlesbrough and Norwich City. His first class career ended at the outbreak of the Second World War. After war service with the RAF he returned to Hucknall to form the successful Linby Colliery side. Later he 'rescued' Notts County Football Club, filling the breach as manager at Meadow Lane on three occasions.

Robert ' Bob' Marshall, 1903-1966. Bob Marshall, third in line, waits to receive his winner's medal at Wembley from King George V, his victorious Manchester City side having beaten Portsmouth 2-1 in the cup final of 1934. Bob Marshall's local club was Hucknall Olympic. At the age of sixten, he left Hucknall to join Sunderland and in 1923, was transferred to Manchester City where he stayed for the rest of his playing career, retiring in 1938. After the Second World War he was appointed manager of Stockport County, later joining Chesterfield Football Club in the same capacity. After retirement from football, he became landlord of the Glapwell Arms, Derbyshire where he died in 1966.

Employees of the Vedonis Factory board the train at the Central Station Hucknall for their annual outing 1936. The Vedonis slogan on the engine boiler states, 'Next to myself I like Vedonis'

Another view of the same outing in 1936. The Vedonis Factory can be seen on the left, presumably empty, as the staff are all on the platform!

Hucknall businessman and motor sportsman Frank Sisson was, in the 1920s, acknowledged as the leader among grass track racers and throughout the Midlands, undisputedly the best. He was employed as works rider for Norton, Ariel and Raleigh, riding in many first class races including The Manx and Dutch tourist races.

Hucknall Byron Boys' Football Club, Albert Street recreation ground, c. 1948. Left to right, standing: Harry Willows, Ray Timmins, Russell Tomlinson, -?-, Colin Hitch, -?-. Front row, Bernard Hitch, Dennis Willows, Keith Cowell, Barry Thorpe, -?-, -?-, John Burton.

A group of bowlers outside the pavilion Titchfield Park in the 1950s. On the extreme left is Eric Johnstone. Mr, Bodill is holding the microphone with Tom Greenhalgh on his left. Third from the left at the back is park keeper Harold Smith.

Two men in a boat. W. Hardstaff (right) takes a friend (name unknown) for a hazardous-looking spin on Titchfield Park Lake in the 1930s.

Papplewick Lido in its heyday in the 1930s. Just a cycle ride away from Hucknall and the place to be on a hot summer's day.

Mr Toon of Bolsover Street displaying ornaments shaped by him from coal.

The Elizabeth Bodill Challenge Cup was the first prize in the Brass Band Contest in the Carnivals of the 1930s. Is it still in the town to-day?

Seven

Get Togethers

Hucknall Band of Hope Union at Welbeck Abbey 18 June 1896.

A group of Hucknall townspeople on the steps of the Palace Theatre Newark in the 1920s where they attended a presentation by people of Newark to Zachariah A. Green who was house surgeon at the town's hospital. Dr Green is in the centre with a bowler hat and gloves. Henry and Ruth Morley stand one behind the other on the left of the group. This a fascinating group picture, particularly for all its 1920's costume interest.

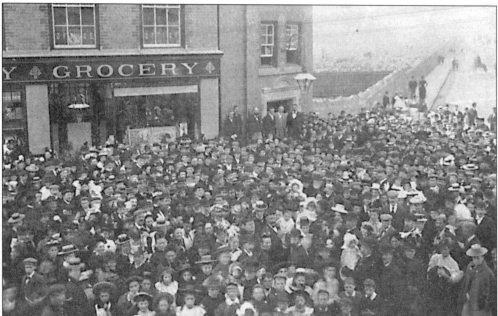

Huge crowds gathered for the opening of the first building stage of the Hucknall Co-operative Society Central Premises in 1898. The entrance to the hall can be seen in the background. Further on up Annesley Road there is the space where the Scala Cinema was later to be built.

Proud citizens pose in front of the new nurses' home which they pioneered to build, in 1897.

Butler's Hill children congregate outside their school at the corner of Hankin Street on Election Day in 1900. The cigar factory can be seen in the background.

A class of children from Spring Street School, *c.* 1916. Headmaster Joseph Barker is on the left of the picture.

95

Liberal Association supporters' garden party in September 1922, at Papplewick Grange, then the home of Sir Julien Cahn. The house was later demolished and the grounds turned into the lido, seen earlier, which in turn has now given way to housing. Left to right, front row: Mrs Harper, Charles Tee (Liberal candidate), Mrs Cahn, Sir Julian and the Revd A.B. Reid (rector of Linby). Immediately behind him is Mr W.J. Calladine.

The Bodill family, 1920s. Joseph Bodill (seated) founded his building and contracting business in Hucknall in 1890 and as his family grew his six sons also joined him in the business. Following a disastrous fire at their Yorke Street Depot in 1922, they built and transferred to the present premises in Sherwood Street. In 1905 the company built the present Dispatch Office works and the adjoining house.

On Tuesday 12 June 1923 Newstead Abbey was the venue for the fourth Installation Festival of the Byron Lodge of Freemasons No. 4014 and Ernest Z. Green was installed as Worshipful Master. The Byron Lodge was consecrated in 1920. The Lodge in the formative years held their meetings first at the Co-operative Hall in Hucknall and then in the Coffee Tavern, moving to the Public Hall in 1923. The Church Hall became their meeting place in 1937 and continued until 1991 when the move to the Mansfield Masonic Hall was made and where the Lodge continues to flourish.

A cheerful group of people await the arrival of the train at the town station in around 1900. Were they off for a day trip or waiting to greet an arrival?

Annesley Hall was the venue for many outdoor meetings and garden parties before its demise. Col. J.N. Chaworth-Musters can be seen at the top of the terrace steps on this occasion addressing a large gathering of people.

The funeral of Joey the Crow, *c.* 1944. This popular bird among the people of Hucknall was laid to rest by its owner Gordon Riley at the family home on Ladycroft Avenue and all the children came to pay their respects.

These two photographs show children's parties in Hucknall in the 1930s but we no longer know what they were celebrating. No doubt the problem will be solved when people recognise friends, family or themselves in the scenes! The one above appears to be a celebration of a national event with its flags and bunting, perhaps the coronation in 1937. The one below looks more like a private party. The girls at the front are very smartly turned out in white gloves and matching satin dresses and headbands!

A street party in George Street, looking towards Annesley Road, probably celebrating one of the post-war victory days.

The backyards have been turned into a party venue with flags and bunting hanging out instead of the washing and everyone is having a great time! 'Hold your ice-creams up for the camera!' These photographs were probably taken on the same occasion as the one opposite.

The tables have been cleared of the food and crockery and there's another opportunity for a group

photograph before everything else is cleared away and the street reverts back to normal.

'All smile for the camera we won't be doing this again for a while!' More street fun in 1937.

A street party in Storth Avenue, thought to be in the mid 1940s and therefore possibly celebrating VE Day.

Eight
Carnivals

Carnival Queen Irene Drakely passes through the town accompanied by her retinue in 1936.

Eric Coates, 'The Uncrowned King of Light Music', returned to the town of his birth to open the carnival in 1935. The composer stands on a platform in the Market Place next to the Carnival Queen, Mabel Morley. Council Chairman Billy Mee stands on the left at the front front, while Lord Byron surveys the scene from his own lofty perch in a niche on the Co-operative buildings behind.

The Carnival Queen Mabel Turton receives her crown, seated on a throne and flanked by her attendants and a page boy with a velvet cushion for her crown in 1934. The platform was erected in front of the parish church.

Carnival Queen Irene Drakely's crowning moment in 1936.

Another 1930's carnival queen, is here being presented with a bouquet by a courteous and immaculatly turned out page boy.

This vast gathering was assembled on the Market Place to witness the opening scenes of the 1938 carnival.

Carnival Queen Betty Noble with a junior assistant helping her with the formalities, 1937.

Audrey Tyler, carnival queen in 1938, receives her crown. The town coat of arms is featured on the back of throne.

The official platform party at the carnival in 1937, Betty Noble was the Queen.

A carnival tableau in Eastwell Street. The mother with the baby on the left is Mrs Clarke and the woman next to the 'policeman' on the right, in a white hat and holding a mallet, is Mrs Albon.

A carnival concert party group from the 1930s. Arthur Saxton, the local wireless shop owner, is at the back in a top hat and his son Eric is on the right wearing a tie.

With a barrel organ in High Street during a carnival in the 1930s. Popular Hucknall newsagent May Bullin is on the right.

An inventive carnival entry by Arthur Saxton who is the one standing on the right of the pair in top hats.

The Hucknall Push Ball competition held during carnival week and being played at the school field in Montague Road.

A carnival crowd watching an event in the Market Place during the 1930s, illustrating the tremendous interest generated by the carnivals at that time. Many of those at the front are in costume. Stallard's shoe establishment can be seen in the background with the Half Moon Hotel towering above it.

Carnival bands assembling on the Market Place before the parade in 1935.

This collection of carnival scenes was assembled as a montage to appear in like this the *Hucknall Dispatch* following the 1938 carnival.

The popular Harlequins Junior Carnival Band marching along South Street in 1935.

The inclement weather seems not to have deterred the crowds at this carnival. This is one of Frank Sissons' famous carnival entries pausing for the photographer in the Market Place.

Mr Joseph Bodill sits in the stocks at this carnival in the 1930s.

Truman Street during carnival week in the 1930s.

Carnival revellers on Linby Top Cross. Bands and groups toured local villages collecting for the carnival charities.

The carnival band marching proudly down Papplewick village Main Street during a tour of local villages in the 1930s.

A panarama of costumed characters, including a row of little 'fusiliers', harlequins and Japanese ladies, assemble on the Market Place for the parade.

A more recent carnival picture. County Councillor Eric Morley poses with the young Hucknall Marching Band members, *c.* 1970.

MODERN DWELLINGS

OF SOUND CONSTRUCTION AND COM-
MON-SENSE DESIGN REPRESENTING THE
EXPERIENCE GAINED IN MANY YEARS
OF HOUSE PLANNING AND ERECTION,
ARE OFFERED TO YOU ON AN IDEAL
AND ELEVATED SITE

Long Hill Rise, Watnall Road (from Watnall Road.

AT

Long Hill Rise Estate

NEAR CENTRAL STATION.

Services include—MAIN SEWER, WATER, GAS, ELECTRICITY, and
CONCRETE CARRIAGE-WAY.   :   :   Inspection without obligation

Prices from £443,

including cost of finished road, and Legal Charges.

Full particulars from office on site or

BODILL & SONS, Ltd.,

BUILDERS.

PORTLAND ROAD, HUCKNALL.   Tel. 45.

The Carnival Magazine of 1936 displayed this advertisement for new houses on Long Hill Rise.

This aerial photograph shows the recently completed Long Hill Rise development advertised above. The Vedonis factory, demolished only quite recently, can just be seen in the bottom left corner.

120

Nine
Preparing for War

Hucknall ladies knitting scarves, socks and blankets for the Forces in 1940. In the picture are (but not necessarily in this order) Mesdames Duffield, Stirland, Calladine, Common, Cupit, Newcombe, Butcher, Bramley, Roberts, Jepson and Stringfellow.

A montage of photographs used in the *Hucknall Dispatch* to show some of the town's preparations at the beginning of the Second World War. At the top is a view of ground being prepared for the construction of air-raid shelters, probably at Broomhill. In the middle picture a loudspeaker car drives down Byron Street, instructing residents to collect their gas masks and at the bottom a queue forms outside Beardall Street infants' school, one of the collection points for gas masks.

Filling sand bags in Yorke Street next to the Dispatch office. Arthur Draper's hairdressing shop can be seen advertising Brylcreem. A lorry owned by H. Tudbury can be seen parked near the wall.

The police station at the junction of Duke Street and Portland Road in wartime garb. Sand bags line the walls and windows and the kerbstones and lamppost base have been painted with white lines to make them show up during the blackouts. This building is now a dental clinic.

Prefabricated houses, or 'prefabs' being delivered to the Gilbert Street site via Watnall Road in the late 1940s. This photograph was taken from what was then Clem Munk's garage. These cheap, emergency houses were originally intended to last for just a few years but in fact remained in use for decades. There are some examples still in use in other parts of the country.

Prefabricated houses in Beardall Street. The roofs of houses in Henry Street can be seen in the distance. The last prefabs remained in Hucknall until well into the 1990s.

This captured German fighter plane was exhibited at the Market Place during the war and proved a magnet to youngsters of the town.

Another wartime composite picture from the *Hucknall Dispatch*, this time on the topic of air-raid shelters. On the left is a view inside the deep shelter that was in Caddaw Avenue and on the right, employees at Richard Richmond's factory, also at Caddaw Avenue, file into the shelters during an air-raid drill.

Newly-built ground level air raid shelters.

Anderson shelters, probably on Byron Street near Highfields Productions factory.

Hucknall Women's Voluntary Service marching to the Market Square. Miss Dorothy Plumb who lived at The Manor in Portland Park is second from the right. The local Boys Brigade can just be seen at the rear of the parade.

Hucknall's 'Dads Army' led by Lt Adrian Toone MM (former headmaster at Spring Street school) proudly swings his men round the top of High Street to assemble on the Market Place.

The town's wartime fire brigade stands ready for action in the Council Yard.

A practice drill for Hucknall's decontamination squad in the early part of the Second World War. All were members of the Hucknall Urban District Health Department but it will be difficult to recognise any of them!